WOODEN FURNITURE HACKS

WOODEN FURNITURE HACKS

OVER 20 STEP-BY-STEP PROJECTS
FOR A UNIQUE AND STYLISH HOME

HESTER VAN OVERBEEK

CICO BOOKS
LONDON NEW YORK

To Ian, Kiki, and Kermit

Published in 2019 by CICO Books
An imprint of Ryland Peters & Small Ltd
20–21 Jockey's Fields   341 E 116th St
London WC1R 4BW   New York, NY 10029

www.rylandpeters.com

10 9 8 7 6 5 4 3 2 1

Projects in this book first appeared in *Furniture Hacks*,
published in 2015

A CIP catalog record for this book is available from the
Library of Congress and the British Library.

ISBN: 978 1 78249 720 2

Printed in China

Editor: Gillian Haslam
Designer: Geoff Borin
Style photographer: James Gardiner
Stylist and step photographer: Hester van Overbeek

Editor: Carmel Edmonds
Art director: Sally Powell
Production controller: Mai-Ling Collyer
Publishing manager: Penny Craig
Publisher: Cindy Richards

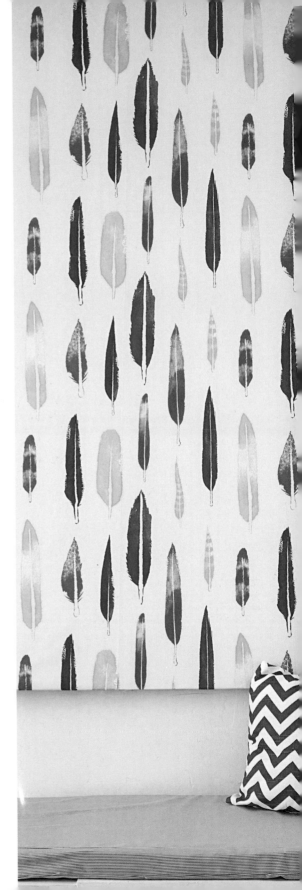

CONTENTS

INTRODUCTION

Welcome to my book and thank you for picking it up! When you flip through the pages, you will find 23 great projects for your home, all made from other items you might already have lying around—as you will see, upcycling and reusing are two of my passions.

The projects are easy to follow and all are relatively easy to make— I always say if I can make it, anyone can! I've been crafting and making things from a young age but, with no formal training (I work as a makeup artist), I'm living proof that anybody can make their own furniture and decorations for their home.

I grew up in a small town in the Dutch countryside. If the weather was too bad to play outside, we sat around the kitchen table crafting—everything from painting and drawing, making clothes for Barbie dolls, and sewing small felt toys to my all-time favorite, drawing interior design sketches for my bedroom. My dad showed me how to do woodwork and painting, while my mum taught me how to use a sewing machine and work with textiles. However, even if you have never made anything in your life before, the step-by-step pictures and instructions in this book will guide you through.

Two years ago, I had the opportunity to decorate a beach house on the south coast of England. This project was way bigger than anything I had ever tackled before, but I loved deciding on the color scheme and picking the furnishings. This house was much bigger then our previous home, so we needed more furniture. My budget wasn't big, so I decided to make most of the furniture myself, and revamp the items we already had to suit my new decorating theme. Believe me, a lot of people asked "Are you sure you can do this?" and remarked "That will never work, just buy it." I was determined to ignore these comments, and my mantra of "Just do it and if it goes wrong, just take it apart and do it again" paid off. The house looked amazing. A friend who came to visit said I should start a blog to show other people how to decorate on a budget, and my website Hester's Handmade Home was born.

I hope this book gives you lots of ideas on how to decorate your home and upcycle some of your old pieces of furniture.

Happy crafting!

Hester X

HESTER'S TIPS

Throughout this book, you'll find heaps of advice, both in the projects and in the tools and techniques section (see pages 102–109), but here are just a few tips and tricks I've learned that will help you as you go along.

Creating a moodboard Before I start a project, I like to create a moodboard. I gather images of styles (e.g. pages torn from magazines and catalogs) and swatches of color that inspire me. When I design furniture, I sketch some drawings. Another great tool is Pinterest—I love using this website to make pinboards.

Finding inspiration Take your inspiration from anything—pictures of nature can inspire paint colors, fashion images can give you ideas about textures. Don't limit yourself to looking at photos of furniture and interiors.

Measuring The saying goes "measure twice, cut once," and this is so true! Always make sure you measure your wood or fabric before you make the first cut. By being accurate at this early stage, you will have a better chance of your project being a big success.

A helping hand Sometimes you will need another pair of hands to hold pieces of wood in position. If you don't have anybody to help you, use masking tape. Line up your pieces of wood and tape in place. You can drill and hammer through the tape and remove it once the join is secure.

Keeping track Sometimes you need to saw a lot of pieces of wood, so to make it easier to remember which piece goes where, mark your wood with a number. Simply stick a little bit of numbered masking tape on your timber and write down its number on a plan of your project.

Opening paint cans Paint cans are very easy to open using a flathead screwdriver. Just move it along the top, gently trying to flip the lid up every inch or so until it pops open.

Making wallpaper level When you paper big surfaces like a wall, draw a straight line the width of your paper on the wall using a spirit level. This ensures your first length of paper is straight and you can use that as a guide for the rest. When papering small surfaces, you don't have to bother with this.

Drawing straight lines Did you know you can use your saw handle to draw a straight line? Put your saw handle against your wood and follow the blade with a pencil. A corner square is also great for drawing straight cutting lines. Hold one side of the square against the wood, and the other side will show you where to draw your line.

Storing your tools I have a tool box but find it is too bulky and heavy to carry around. I like collecting together all the tools I need for a project and placing them in a plastic tub. When you complete your project, you can place everything back and your house/workspace stays tidy.

CHAPTER 1
LIVING ROOM

WALLPAPER CANVAS

Large statement paintings can really make a room, but they come at a cost—so wouldn't it be good to make something yourself for a fraction of the price? The artwork I made here is huge, but you can scale it down. You could create a collection of small canvases and display them close together as a collage, make a medium-sized one for a small wall, or go even bigger than I did for massive impact. This project is a great way to use up leftover rolls of wallpaper—the end result looks impressive but is easy to make, just the way we like it!

YOU WILL NEED

- wooden batten, length depending on the size of your canvas
- measuring tape
- saw
- miter box
- wood glue
- wood screws
- screwdriver
- canvas or other sturdy fabric (see tip on page 12), slightly larger than your frame
- staple gun
- wallpaper paste
- wallpapering brush
- leftover roll of wallpaper
- wallpaper smoother
- scissors
- picture frame D rings and screws

CREATING THE FRAME

1 Decide on the dimensions for your canvas (make sure that you have enough fabric and wallpaper to cover the whole frame and to wrap around the sides) and cut your batten accordingly. For my canvas, I cut two 71 in (180cm) lengths and two 59 in (150cm) lengths.

2 Cut four corner pieces to stabilize the frame. I used up offcuts so they are slightly different lengths, but aim for an approximate length of 8 in (20cm). You will need to miter-cut the ends of the offcuts, as they have to be at a 45-degree angle (see page 105). Make sure that the two ends of each offcut are sawn in opposing directions in order to butt up to the frame—see photo.

3 Put the frame together by gluing and then screwing the joints together (just one screw in the middle of the joint will suffice).

4 Add the corner pieces, attaching them in a similar way with a little glue at the end and one screw to keep in place.

TIP
I used a sturdy canvas as my frame is pretty big, but for a smaller canvas you could use part of an old sheet or even a T-shirt.

5 Lay the fabric flat on the floor with the frame on top. Cut the fabric so that you have an additional 3 in (7.5cm) exra on all sides. Fold the top of the fabric over the frame and attach it to the fabric with a staple gun. Staple along the entire length of the top batten. Move to the center of the other end of the frame, pull the fabric as tight as you can, and staple in place, then continue to staple the whole length of the batten.

6 Wrap the fabric around the corners (just like you would wrap a present) and staple in place. Continue stapling the sides, making sure the fabric is pulled tight to make a strong canvas.

TIP

If you wish, rather than using just one wallpaper design, you could use up different wallpaper patterns to create a collage or patchwork of varying prints.

PAPERING THE CANVAS

7 Mix up the wallpaper paste according to the packet instructions and smear it over the canvas. Stick on the first piece of wallpaper, positioning it so that you have enough paper overhang to wrap around the top, bottom, and sides of the frame.

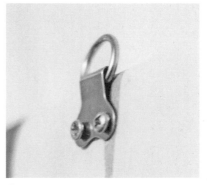

8 Use a clean brush and wallpaper smoother to remove any bubbles under the paper (see page 108). Try to stick the paper on as smoothly as possible—it's trickier papering a canvas than a wall as the fabric will move a little, but be patient and you will get a good result. If working on a big canvas, you will need to add a second, third, or even fourth length of paper —make sure the patterns align perfectly for a seamless effect.

9 When the front is papered, carefully turn the canvas around and paste the sides, top, and bottom of the frame. Smooth the paper over the frame and wrap the corners as if wrapping a present. If your paper needs a bit of extra support, use a few staples on the back of the frame once the paper is dry. Trim off any excess bits of paper.

10 Screw the hanging supports to the top of the frame—I used two picture frame D rings that hang from screws attached to the wall. If you cannot drill holes in your wall, simply leave your canvas resting against the wall.

MAGAZINE TABLE

I love magazines—there's just something so relaxing about flicking through a new magazine with a steaming mug of hot coffee. Magazines inspire me not only with their interior stories, but also with the textures and colors on the fashion pages, the beautiful still-life food photography, and fascinating articles about creative people. This obsession means that each month I buy yet more magazines. As I find it impossible to throw them away, I came up with this fun way of storing them.

YOU WILL NEED

- stack of magazines
- leftover piece of wood, MDF (medium-density fiberboard), or board
- pen
- saw
- sandpaper
- paint
- paintbrush
- small caster wheels
- small wood screws
- screwdriver
- piece of glass the same size as your magazines (I used glass from an old picture frame)
- binding twine or yarn

1 Gather together a stack of magazines. They need to be roughly the same size and, ideally, with the same binding color—for this project I chose white.

2 Measure out the base of the table by placing your largest magazine on the piece of wood and trace around it. Cut out the rectangle (I like to use a hand saw, but you could use an electric one).

3 Sand the rough edges of the base and paint it. I chose white to give the magazine stack a fresh feel. You don't need to paint it too neatly, as most of the base will be covered with magazines—just make sure the sides are done thoroughly.

4 Attach the caster wheels to the base by screwing them in with little wood screws. Space them equidistantly so your table is stable.

5 Start stacking, aligning your magazines as neatly as possible and as high as you like. My table is 12 in (30cm) high—if you go higher than this, it would be good to glue the magazines together for extra stability. You can also improve stability by putting the odd magazine the wrong way around, so the pages face you instead of the binding.

6 Make your top magazine or page a beautiful one as this is the image that will be on view all the time. If you don't like seeing the cover with all its type, opt for a stunning photo as I did here.

7 Clean both sides of the glass if necessary and lay it on top of your magazine stack. Remember that glass has sharp edges and is breakable, so this isn't a child-friendly table.

8 Wrap the twine tightly around your magazine stack in several places to hold it all together, and tie in a secure knot.

TIP
If you wish, you can make a matching stool! Tie the stack of magazines tightly, but don't add the pane of glass.

JERSEY ROPE FOOTSTOOL

I love giving a modern twist to something old-fashioned, and a good example of this type of hacking is this footstool. It looked tatty and unloved, but changing its seat from the old rattan to a brightly colored chunky yarn gave the stool a new lease of life. Any footstool with a fabric or rattan seat can be given a makeover—you might have a similar piece of furniture in your attic or you can pick them up for next to nothing in secondhand furniture stores or on eBay, which is where I found mine.

YOU WILL NEED

- old footstool
- scissors
- sandpaper
- paint and paintbrush (optional)
- chunky yarn (I used Zpagetti yarn, and this footstool required approximately 55 yards/50m)

TIP

I love working with Zpagetti yarn—it's made from cotton leftovers from the fashion industry, and the clever people at Hoooked (see page 110) turn it into big spools of yarn that you can use for all kinds of home crafts. Alternatively, a thick yarn would also work well.

1 Cut away the stool's original seating. I tried to keep as much of the twine intact as possible because I intended to use it for another project (see Updated drawer handles, page 60). There's no need to clean the footstool as the wood will be sanded later.

2 Continue removing all the twine or rattan until you are left with just the wooden frame.

3 Sand the wood down to remove any old varnish or paint. After sanding, I liked the color of the wood so much that I decided to leave it in its natural state, but at this stage you could paint the frame any color you like.

4 Take your ball of Zpagetti or other strong yarn. Tie the end of the yarn securely to one of the upper side bars of the stool.

5 Wrap the yarn across the seat, from one side to the other, taking it over the top of the frame and then across the underside. The yarn needs to be pulled taut.

6 Keep wrapping until you have covered the whole width of the seat. Make sure that the total number of wraps is a multiple of five, e.g. 50, 55, or 60 wraps, depending on the size of the stool frame.

7 Move the ball of yarn over to one of the side bars, and wrap it once around the bar to secure it in place.

8 Now weave the yarn up and over every five strands. To start, go under the first five strands, then up and over the next five strands. Continue this under/over process until you reach the other side of the frame. Go back in the opposite direction, so over where you went under, and under where you went over. Push the wraps of yarn up close together to create a stronger seat, and remember to keep the yarn pulled taut.

TIP
As you weave the yarn up and over, if you wish you can create a pattern—instead of alternating every under/over wrap, you can have several rows of the same direction next to each other.

9 Keep going until you have woven the whole stool seating. It's better to work with a small ball of yarn as this is easier to push through the strands—I cut a length of around 11 yards (10m) and rolled it into a small ball.

10 If you run out of yarn, simply tie the end of the old piece securely to the new length of yarn and keep weaving. Any knots or loose ends can be pushed through to the underside.

11 When you have finished, cut the yarn and tie it securely to a side post. Tuck the tail end to the underside.

MODULAR BOOKCASE

This bookcase doubles up as a display case. I made it from pieces of MDF, but you can create something similar from old wooden crates or boxes. If you wish to store heavy items, use thicker wood or MDF. The boxes are stacked on top of each other, creating a large storage space which can easily be reconfigured into a different shape. To make the bookcase secure, I screwed my boxes together and anchored the finished structure to the wall. I can still move the small cubes about whenever I fancy a change.

YOU WILL NEED

- measuring rule
- pencil and paper
- leftover pieces of MDF (medium-density fiberboard) or readymade boxes
- saw
- wood glue
- masking tape
- hammer
- nails
- wood screws
- screwdriver
- corner brackets
- drill
- wall plugs
- paint (I used a white milk paint)
- paintbrush

1 Measure how long, wide, and deep you want your bookcase to be. Mine is built into an alcove and I made it 12 in (30cm) deep. Make a drawing of squares and rectangles to see what would work well in your room. If you have any large items you wish to store or display, make sure that the cubes are a suitable size. Work out how many boxes you need, or how much MDF you need to buy.

2 Cut the MDF to shape or have this done by your local home improvement or do-it-yourself store (this will save you a lot of sawing and measuring!). It's a good idea to label the pieces at this stage to make assembling the cubes easier.

3 To assemble the cubes, apply wood glue to the edge of your wood, place it in position, and press it down. Always double-check you are attaching the correct pieces together before you apply the glue.

4 Apply strips of masking tape to hold the cube together, then hammer nails into the joins.

5 When assembling larger cubes, it's helpful to position a stool or chair under the MDF to support it and keep it in place while you hammer in the nails.

6 Make all your cubes and rectangles in this way.

7 Stack your finished pieces on top of each other. To make the bookcase more secure, screw the big pieces together using small wood screws. Also, anchor the bookcase to the wall by screwing a couple of corner brackets to the underside of a shelf and to the wall (use wall plugs).

8 Paint your bookcase any color you like. I chose white, as this ties in with the wall and means the bookcase doesn't dominate the room. If you want your color to stand out, use a primer first. I just gave mine two coats of white paint, allowing the first coat to dry properly before applying the second.

TIP

If you wish to make the bookcase from pre-made boxes, ask a wine merchant if they have any wine boxes for sale, or a grocery store for apple or vegetable boxes. You may have to smooth any rough edges with sandpaper before assembling the bookcase.

WASHI TAPE CHEST

Painting furniture can seem daunting, as once you have painted a piece of wood, it feels like there is no way back. (There is, of course, but it involves a lot of sanding!) In addition, you might not know which colors you want to live with, so testing out a non-permanent color scheme can only be good. In these cases, cue the washi tape! This tape is easy to remove, so it's the perfect partner for the craft beginner or the fickle of mind. Simply stick the tape to a chest of drawers to create great geometric patterns that almost look painted on.

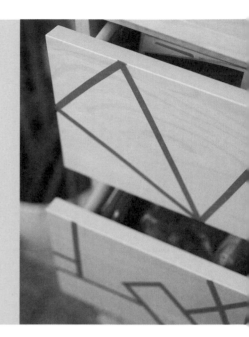

YOU WILL NEED
- chest of drawers
- washi tape
- scissors

1 Gather together your tapes—I use washi tape a lot, so I keep the reels close to hand in a big basket on my desk.

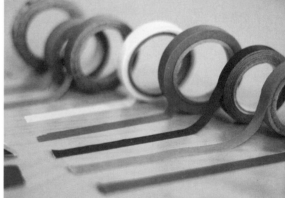

2 Have a look at which colors go well together. Here I'm decorating four drawers, so I want four colors that complement each other. By lining up the reels of tape next to each other, you can decide which combinations you like best.

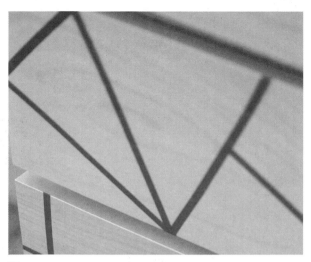

3 Start sticking lengths of tape to your drawer, making different sized triangles, squares, and other geometric shapes.

4 Press the tape on by sliding your finger over it. Washi tape is made from paper and sometimes needs a little help adhering correctly.

5 Cut the ends of the tape in neat straight lines for a professional finish.

6 Simply repeat the process on the remaining drawers, using different colored tapes to complete your design.

CHAPTER 2

KITCHEN AND DINING ROOM

TWO-CHAIR BENCH

Doesn't this bench look utterly charming? And who would guess that it started life as two dining chairs? You can use two identical chairs, as I did, or give your bench more character by using different chairs (just make sure the seats are the same height). I will explain the stages for making this chair bench, but it's not possible to give exact measurements for the wooden seat and backrest as this depends on the chairs you use. When it comes to painting, get creative with different colors—I went for an ombré effect and used three shades of blue.

YOU WILL NEED

- two dining chairs
- saw
- measuring tape
- smooth planed wood, 1⁵⁄₁₆ x ¾ in (34 x18mm), for the frame
- sandpaper
- thicker wood, for the seat and backrest
- four corner brackets
- electric drill
- screws
- screwdriver
- C clamp
- quick-drying filler
- filling knife
- paint and paintbrush

DISMANTLING THE OLD CHAIRS

1 Select two chairs that are either the same style or have their seats at the same height. If possible, remove the seat pad—if you turn the chair upside down, you will see the screws holding it in place.

2 You only need to use the backs of the chairs, so you have to take them apart. If using modern chairs, you might be able to unscrew the backs. However, for older chairs, such as the ones shown here, use a saw and carefully cut through the side seat supports.

BUILDING THE NEW SEAT

3 Also saw through any lower supports between the front and back legs. You might have to use gentle force to get the chair apart, but be careful not to break it.

4 Measure the width of your chair and decide on the dimensions of your bench. The depth of the bench seat is determined by the width of the chair back. The chairs I used are 14½ in (37cm) wide and I wanted my bench to be 33½ in (85cm) long.

5 To build the frame of the bench, measure and cut four pieces of smooth planed wood—you will need two pieces measuring the width of your chair and two the desired length. For my bench, that is two 14½ in (37cm) pieces and two 33½ in (85cm) pieces. Sand the rough edges once cut.

6 Join the frame using the four corner brackets, making sure all the corners are right angles.

7 Attach the frame securely to the chair backs, holding it in position with a C clamp while you use the screwdriver. Don't place the screws all in a straight line—alternating them up and down a little means there is less chance of the timber splitting.

8 Attach the frame to the second chair back in exactly the same way.

9 For the seat, you can use wood of varying widths but it must be of the same thickness. I like to use whatever I have left over from other projects, so, as you can see, my pieces of wood are all different.

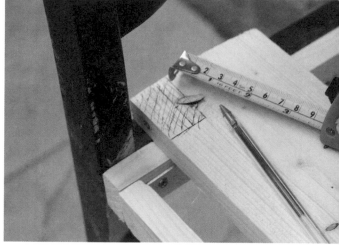

10 The front and back pieces of wood will probably each need a little square cut out at the corner to allow them to fit snugly to the chair backs. Measure, mark, and saw the square out.

11 Measure and cut more wood to length until you have filled the frame.

12 To attach the wood to the frame, predrill holes in the wood slightly bigger than the screws you will use (see page 106). This means the screws disappear once screwed in, giving a smoother finish. Screw the wood to the short and long sides of your frame.

13 To make the seating a little stronger, add two supporting pieces of wood under the seating. Measure precisely so the wood fits snugly, cut to size, and fix in place by drilling a hole slightly larger than the screw and screw in place.

FINISHING AND PAINTING

14 Attach the backrest. Measure how long your wood needs to be and cut to size. I added two backrests using wood of different widths. Screw into the backs of the chairs using wood screws.

15 Fill all the drilled holes and other cracks or damaged areas with filler, using a filling knife. Allow to dry, then smooth down with sandpaper.

16 Also sand the original chair backs—the smoother they are, the easier it will be to paint the bench.

17 Your bench is now ready to be painted (I gave mine an all-over coat of white). Apply a second and maybe even a third coat of paint, depending on how dark your wood is. Allow to dry thoroughly between coats.

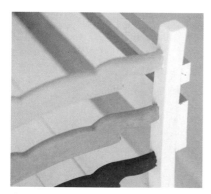

18 You can leave your bench one color or get creative with multiple colors, an ombré effect, or stripes. I painted the sides three shades of blue, from dark to light. To tie in the backrest, I painted the top of the wood two shades of blue as I thought the whole backrest in blue would have looked a bit too heavy. Let the paint dry, then sit back and relax.

Driftwood door handles

Change the look of your cupboards in less than an hour simply by replacing the old handles with pieces of driftwood. You can, of course, scour the beach for suitable pieces, which would make a fun day out, but the other option is to look online. eBay is a great place to find driftwood that has already dried out and been debugged, as doing this yourself will take time. I ordered pieces approximately 6 in (15cm) in length, so all my handles are roughly the same size. Driftwood is very brittle which means you might have to replace or reattach any well-used handles after six months or so.

YOU WILL NEED
- driftwood, ideally straight pieces a minimum of 6 in (15cm) long
- screwdriver
- wood screws

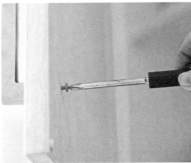

1 Carefully unscrew the old cupboard handles. You may be able to reuse the screws to attach the new handles.

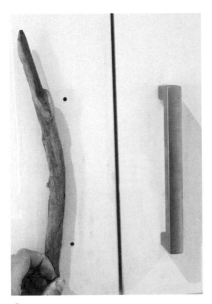

2 Select a piece of driftwood that fits neatly over the existing screw holes in the door.

3 Place a screw in the hole on the reverse side of the door and screw into the piece of driftwood.

4 That's it, your handle is attached! It really couldn't be any easier.

UPDATED CHAIR

Mismatched chairs around a dining table, especially in a plain setting like this all-white room, make a strong style statement. One of the great things about having chairs that are not a set is that you can pick them up for next to nothing. This bargain buy started out unloved and out-of-date, but with a lick of paint and some new fabric it is transformed into a unique chair. An all-over pink chair might be a bit much in this understated room, but painting the legs white allows the back to add a great pop of color without being overwhelming.

YOU WILL NEED

- chair
- screwdriver
- sandpaper
- cloth
- two colors of paint
- paintbrushes
- varnish (optional)
- two large pieces of batting (wadding)
- scissors
- staple gun
- fabric
- upholstery nails
- hammer

PAINTING THE CHAIR

1 First remove the seat padding. Use a screwdriver to ease out the old upholstery nails or staples—be careful as they may be rusty and could break.

2 Sand the chair all over to remove any chipped paint. Brush the chair to remove any dust and wipe down with a cloth.

3 Give the chair its first coat of paint. I used coral pink on the back rest and white on the legs. There is no need to paint the entire seat, as this will be covered by fabric, but continue the paint around the base of the backrest spokes. Let the paint dry thoroughly, then give your chair a second coat. Apply a third coat if necessary.

4 When the paint has dried, if you wish, apply a coat of varnish to protect your paintwork and give the chair a nice shine.

MAKING THE CUSHION

5 For a well-padded seat, use thick batting and fold it over several times.

6 Drape a longer piece of batting over the folded piece—this needs to be large enough to wrap over to the underside of the chair seat.

7 Starting from the back of the chair, staple the batting in place using a staple gun.

8 Fold the batting under the chair and staple securely in place.

9 Drape your fabric over the seat. If using a patterned fabric like mine, make sure you position the fabric so that the design or writing is centered. Trim the fabric so that it covers the seat and sides, with a 3 in (7.5cm) overhang.

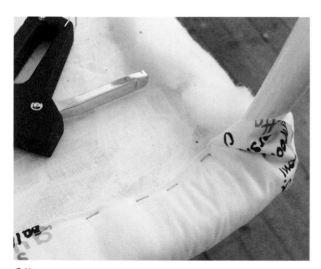

10 Fold the fabric over to hide the raw edges and secure in place with the staple gun. Try to make the edges as neat as possible.

11 For a professional finish, cover the staples on the chair seat with a row of upholstery nails. To avoid hammer marks on the white nails, place a piece of fabric between the nail and the hammer.

KITCHEN ISLAND

Kitchen islands are expensive, so why not make your own from an old cabinet or chest of drawers? With an all-white base you can get creative with the details—I added a splash of citrus to the sides of the drawers and gave the inside shelf a coat of peacock blue. For the worktop, I found this fabulous old wooden sign. While looking for a piece of wood at my local junk yard, I stumbled upon this sign; originally it wasn't for sale as it was still in use, but for the right price and a friendly smile it was mine.

YOU WILL NEED

- old cabinet or chest of drawers
- screwdriver
- saw
- quick-drying filler and filling knife
- sandpaper
- paint
- paintbrush
- worktop (see step 7 for details and dimensions)
- very strong glue, such as No More Nails
- two wooden brackets
- screws
- drawer handles or, as used here, boat cleats
- nuts and bolts to attach the handles
- drill
- clear varnish
- four caster wheels

PREPARING THE ISLAND

1 Find a suitable cabinet or chest of drawers—ideally you want some shelves and drawers. Remove any cabinet doors by unscrewing the hinges and take out the drawers. Remove any drawer handles or knobs.

TIP

An offcut piece of butcher's block would look great on top of the island too—have a look in your local kitchen store or wood supplier. Gumtree or eBay are also good places to find reasonably priced wood offcuts, as you can always find people selling leftover bits of kitchen builds there. Can't find any reclaimed wood you like? Use a thick sheet of MDF (medium-density fiberboard) painted your favorite color instead.

2 Remove the legs from the cabinet. They might be screwed, nailed, or glued on, so unscrew, saw, or pull the legs off but be careful not to damage the cabinet.

3 Fill all the holes left by the hinges, knobs, and screws with quick-drying filler. When it has dried, smooth with sandpaper.

TIP

If you have to give your furniture several coats of paint, wrap your paintbrushes in aluminum foil while you wait for the paint to dry. This prevents the paint on the brush drying, so you don't have to keep washing your brushes in between applying coats.

PAINTING THE ISLAND

4 Give your cabinet a base coat of paint, including the inside. There is no need to paint the top as this will be covered by the new worktop.

5 For a fun accent, paint the sides of the drawers a different color—I chose lime and yellow. These colors aren't on view all the time, so they are not in your face but they do give a little pop whenever you open the drawers.

6 Give your cabinet its second and maybe third coat of paint, allowing the coats to dry between each application. My cabinet was made from a very dark wood, so it needed three coats of paint.

7 The new worktop needs to be at least 8 in (20cm) wider and 10 in (25cm) longer than the top of your cabinet. This can be an old wooden sign like mine, a piece of butcher's block, a thick sheet of MDF, or a leftover piece of kitchen worktop. Apply very strong glue to the top of the cabinet and place the worktop on top. Position the worktop so that the 8 in (20cm) of extra width overhangs at the front of the cabinet.

TIP

If using MDF for your worktop, paint it using an all-in-one paint to avoid having to prime it first.

ADDING THE WORKTOP

8 Weigh down the worktop evenly (I used piles of heavy books) to help the glue set.

9 To help support the worktop, I added wooden brackets under the overhang. As my cabinet has a little ledge on top, I had to cut out a square of wood. Measure the depth and height of the ledge and use a saw to create this notch in the bracket. If you are lucky, your cabinet won't have this and you can skip this step.

10 Attach your brackets under the overhang of the worktop using the glue. Also screw them in from inside the cabinet. Give the underside of the worktop and the brackets a lick of paint.

FINISHING TOUCHES

11 For the drawer handles, I wanted my island to have a slight industrial feel so opted for steel boat cleats, but you could also choose ceramic knobs or metal bars. Drill a hole in your drawer and select a bolt long enough to go through your handle and the drawer. Secure in place with a nut inside the drawer.

12 Give your worktop a coat of clear varnish. This will make the worksurface easier to clean and if you opted for the MDF top, this will make the paint last longer. My wooden sign was slightly weathered, so I gave it four coats of varnish, letting it dry completely between coats.

13 Attach caster wheels to the bottom of the island. Mine are 4 in (10cm) high and the metal matches the drawer handles. Make sure the wheels you choose can carry the weight of the island plus all the stuff you will store in it.

PATTERNED TILE TRAY

This project will teach you two new skills. First you make the patterned tiles, then you build a tray around them. I love patterned tiles but they are expensive, so luckily it's really easy to make your own using inexpensive tiles, patterned paper, and varnish glue. The glue makes the tiles hardwearing—you can even clean them with a wet cloth. For the tray I used offcuts of MDF leftover from another project, but wood would work just as well. You can make a square or rectangular tray, depending on how many tiles you have to play with.

YOU WILL NEED

- tiles
- paper
- scissors
- varnish glue, such as Mod Podge
- sponge applicator
- offcuts of wood or MDF (medium-density fiberboard)
- drill with wood bit
- electric saw
- sandpaper
- wood glue
- hammer
- small nails or panel pins
- masking tape
- paint (I used milk paint in a coral shade)
- paintbrush
- strong glue, such as No More Nails

COVERING THE TILES

1 Gather together a lot of paper with nice prints. I have a whole box of pages I have torn out of magazines that I find inspiring or that have amazing photos on them. Lots of craft magazines also have special editions that feature fabulous patterned sheets of paper ideal for use in this project.

2 Select your favorite pieces of paper and cut them a little larger than your tile, so that they will wrap around the sides. Apply a generous amount of varnish glue to the tile with a sponge applicator and stick the paper on top, with an even overhang of paper on all sides. Smooth the paper down with the sponge applicator to ensure there are no air bubbles.

3 Apply a layer of varnish glue on top of the paper and stick the extra bits of paper around the sides of the tile, making them as smooth as possible.

4 Make all your tiles this way. When the varnish glue has dried, apply another two coats, allowing them to dry thoroughly between applications.

TIP

When cutting out the handles (see step 5), you may find it is easier to measure the end pieces and mark the cutting lines, then measure and cut out the handles, and then cut the end pieces to size. It can be easier to cut the holes on a bigger piece of wood.

MAKING THE TRAY

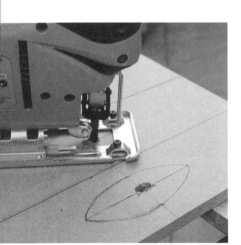

5 Cut the wood to size: **Base:** measure the length and width of your tray base by butting the tiles closely together on the piece of wood and draw around them. Cut the tray base to size. **Short end pieces (where the handles go):** I decided to make my tray 2¾ in (7cm) high, but you can adjust this if you wish. Measure two pieces of wood 2¾ in (7cm) by the width of your tray. **Long side pieces:** Measure two pieces 2¾ in (7cm) by the length of your tray plus the width of the two end pieces (the wood I used is ½ in/ 1cm thick, so I added this measurement twice to the length). To cut out the handles, find the middle of the end piece and mark dots 2 in (5cm) either side of the middle and dots ¾ in (2cm) above and below the middle. Join the dots up to create an oval shape—this will be your handle. Drill a hole in the middle of the handle and using an electric saw, saw out the handle pieces to leave an oval hole. Cut out the end and side pieces.

6 Sand all the cut edges of the base, sides, and ends until they are smooth.

7 Apply wood glue to one end of the base. Place an end piece in position and nail through the bottom of the side piece into the base. It can help to use masking tape to hold the pieces in position. Repeat with the other end piece.

8 Glue the side pieces to the tray in the same way.

9 Nail the side pieces to the base and to the end pieces.

TIP

The patterned tiles also make great coasters, or stick them to a tabletop for a unique effect—I even used them on a kitchen island.

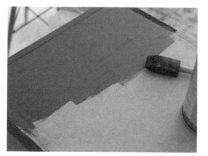

10 Now you can paint your tray —I used milk paint, which doesn't require a primer. Paint the base and the sides first. Once these are dry, flip the tray over and paint the inside. Don't bother painting the inside of the base, as this will be hidden by the tiles. When dry, apply a second coat if necessary.

11 Apply the strong glue to the tray base and stick the tiles in place. Place something heavy in the tray (such as a big stack of books) to weigh the tiles down and ensure they adhere correctly. Leave to dry for the time stated on the glue tube. There is no need to grout between the tiles, as they will fit snugly. Give the tiles one final coat of varnish glue for extra protection.

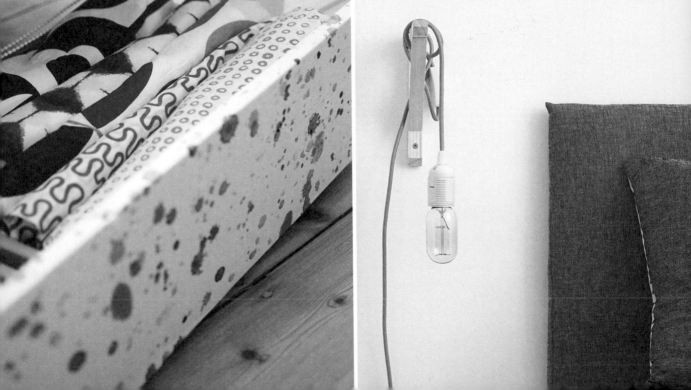

CHAPTER 3
BEDROOM

FOUR-POSTER BED

This bed looks impressive, but is fairly easy to put together! You can adapt the measurements and quantity of wood to suit any bed with a square base. Have you noticed the shelf behind the bed? I don't like bedside tables as they take up too much room, but the shelf gives you a display area without occupying floor space. I also added hidden shelves behind the bed to keep books close to hand. For the canopy, I used soft white for a nautical look, but you could use patterned fabric for nomad style, or drape sheers from all four posts for a romantic feel.

YOU WILL NEED

- bed with a wooden base and headboard (mine is an Ikea Malm)
- four beams, 2⁵⁄₁₆ x 2¾ x 83 in (6 x 7 x 210cm)—these form the upright posts
- plank of reclaimed wood, approximately 6 in (15cm) deep and the width of your bed—this forms the shelf
- spirit level
- smaller offcuts of reclaimed wood—these form the hidden bookshelves

- four pieces of smooth planed wood ¾ x 2¾ in (2 x 7cm), two the length of the bed and two the width of the bed—these form the top beams
- sandpaper
- three large corner brackets to attach the shelf
- four corner brackets to attach the bookshelves
- eight corner brackets to attach the top beams to the uprights
- wood glue

- saw
- screwdriver
- long and standard wood screws
- drill
- two thin pieces of batten, the width of your bed or slightly narrower
- paint and paintbrush
- thin cotton or muslin, the length of your bed plus an overhang at each end
- thread
- sewing machine

1 Remove the mattress from the bed and pull the bed away from the wall. Start by attaching two upright posts to the headboard. Predrill holes through the posts (see page 106) and use long wood screws to fix the posts to the headboard. I used three screws per post, placing them in a straight line 2 in (5cm), 4 in (10cm), and 10 in (25cm) from the bottom of the post. Make sure the posts line up with the edges of the bed.

2 Saw the reclaimed plank of wood to the same length as the headboard. You also need to measure and cut out a square so that the plank fits neatly around the upright post. Sand away any rough edges.

3 Attach three large corner brackets to the plank, placing two 4 in (10cm) in from the outside edges and one in the middle. Screw the brackets into the headboard, using a spirit level to ensure that the shelf is level.

4 To create the hidden bookshelf, cut a 12 in (30cm) length of wood for the base of the shelf, cutting out a square notch to fit around the upright post, as in step 2. Screw a large and a smaller corner bracket to the underside of the shelf. Fix the shelf to the headboard by screwing in the brackets.

5 Measure the distance between the short, lower shelf and the long, upper shelf and cut another plank to serve as a bookshelf end, to ensure books don't disappear behind the bed. Apply some wood glue along one long edge and one short edge and press the shelf into place with the glued edges against the headboard and the lower shelf. For extra strength, screw in place with a couple of wood screws. Repeat steps 4 and 5 to make another shelf for the other side of the bed.

6 Attach the remaining two upright posts to the foot end of the bed, once again making sure they line up neatly to the edges of the bed. Drill holes and secure with long wood screws.

7 Measure the space between the upright posts at the head and foot of the bead. Cut two pieces of smooth planed wood to this length between the two posts (this should be the length of your bed). Attach in place with corner brackets (it helps to have someone else to hold the wood in place while you use the screwdriver).

8 To complete the four-poster shape, measure the width of the bed, cut the remaining two pieces of planed wood to this length and attach to the uprights with corner brackets.

9 Paint your existing bed and its new frame whatever color you like. I chose a white gloss, but left the shelf unpainted as the reclaimed wood was so attractive. My bed needed three coats of paint because the bed base was quite dark, but you may find two coats will suffice. Allow the paint to dry thoroughly between coats.

10 To make the canopy, take a piece of cotton or muslin the length of the bed plus enough extra fabric to create an overhang at the head and foot of the bed. At each end create a sleeve to house the batten (you can either paint the batten white or leave it as natural wood). Fold over a ½ in (1cm) hem, then fold over again to create a tube large enough to accommodate the batten. Pin and machine stitch in place. Slide the batten through the tube, gathering the fabric slightly to create a pretty ruched effect. Hang the fabric over the front and back beams above the bed.

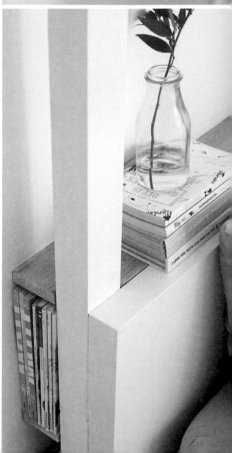

WOODEN BED SURROUND

I love log cabin style, but reclaimed wooden beds can cost an absolute fortune. This project shows you the cheat's way to re-create the look at a fraction of the price. For my guest bedroom, I bought an inexpensive divan bed and then constructed this wooden surround. All my guests are very impressed when I say I built it myself. And as this bed is tucked away in the corner of the room, I only had to build half a surround! If your bed is in the middle of the room, you'll need to build a full surround, but even this can be done in a day.

YOU WILL NEED

- wood—for a double bed, I used five ¾ x 2¾ in (2 x 7cm) pieces, each 95 in (240cm) long
- pallet wood—I cut up four pallets and sanded the wood smooth
- measuring rule
- saw
- strong wood glue
- lots of wood screws
- screwdriver
- electric sander
- damp cloth
- clear varnish and brush (optional)

MAKING THE SIDE AND FOOT PANELS

TIP

I used the wood from four reclaimed pallets for this bed. I took the pallets apart, sanded the wood, and treated it against fungi, as the pallets had been left outside for months. To save time and effort, try to find clean pallets that have only been used indoors.

1 Remove the mattress from the bed base. Decide how large a surround you need to build—my bed is in a corner, so I made a side panel, foot panel, and headboard. First make a frame for the side of your bed—measure the length and height of the bed base, then cut one piece of timber the length of the bed base and eight pieces the height of the bed base. Construct the frame by screwing the short lengths to the longer piece, placing one at each end and spacing the remaining six pieces inbetween at regular intervals.

2 Fill the frame horizontally with pallet wood. It looks good to use wood of different lengths, so you may have to saw some pieces to complete this wooden jigsaw. Butt the pieces up tightly and use strong wood glue and small wood screws to attach them to the frame.

3 When the entire side panel is complete, finish the top of the frame by adding lengths of pallet wood along the top edge, gluing and screwing in place.

4 Measure and construct the foot panel in exactly the same way as for the side panel. When measuring the width of the bed base, add on the width of the side panel.

5 Screw the foot panel and the side panel together with a vertical row of wood screws, screwing from the foot panel into the end of the side panel.

MAKING THE HEADBOARD

6 Measure the height you want the headboard to be—mine is 51 in (130cm) high. Cut two pieces of wood to this length (these will be the uprights), plus three pieces of wood the same length as the foot panel (these will be the horizontal pieces). To join the frame together, lay the two uprights on the floor the correct distance apart. Place the three horizontals between them—the bottom piece needs to be 8 in (20cm) above the height of the bed base, the top piece is level with the top of the uprights, and the middle piece is equidistant between the two. Screw through the horizontals into the uprights. Fill the headboard frame with pieces of pallet wood, this time placing them vertically. Screw them into the frame with small wood screws.

TIP

You may have noticed that I ran out of wood when making the headboard frame and used an old floorboard as one of the horizontal pieces. I don't like a uniform look, so I made sure that the top edges of the wood are at different levels. If you prefer a neater look, align the top edges of the wood.

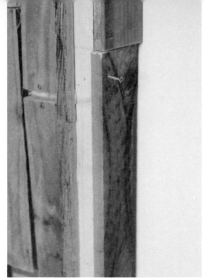

7 Attach the legs of your headboard to the frame of the side panel by screwing through the lower part of the headboard upright into the side panel frame. If you have only one side panel, the weight of the bed will keep the other side of the headboard standing.

8 To hide the side frame of the headboard, cover it with leftover bits of pallet wood, sawing them to the correct size as necessary. Screw the pallet wood to the frame using small wood screws.

SANDING AND FINISHING

9 Cover the front of the headboard frame in the same way. I think it looks good if these pallet wood pieces are the same width as the pieces covering the top of the side frame, as this gives a more cohesive look.

10 Give the bed surround a thorough sanding with the electric sander (see page 106). This might take you at least an hour, but don't skimp on this stage as you don't want any splintery edges. Wipe over with a damp cloth to remove any dust.

11 You can either leave the wood in this untreated state or, if you want to give the bed surround a glossy appearance, give it a coat of clear varnish. Allow the varnish to dry thoroughly before you replace the mattress.

UPDATED DRAWER HANDLES

Many chests of drawers have a generic appearance, but luckily it's super easy to give this essential piece of furniture a more unique look by changing the handles. You could use readymade handles, but isn't it more fun to make your own? Pebbles and stones make great handles and here I'll show you how in three different ways, two with pebbles and one with twine. I'm lucky enough to live by a beach, so there are plenty of pebbles to choose from—ones with holes worn through them are particularly useful.

YOU WILL NEED

- chest of drawers (mine is an Ikea Malm)
- stones or pebbles
- rattan cord or twine
- glue gun
- measuring rule
- drill with wood drill bit

1 When selecting stones or pebbles, consider their size—if they are too large, their weight means they will be difficult to attach, and if they are too small, it will be difficult to open the drawers. The ideal size is around 3–4 in (7–10cm) long and 1¼–2 in (3–5cm) wide.

TIP

I used two different stones for the handles—gray flint and white chalk. It's tricky drilling holes in chalk stone as it's so brittle, so it's better to find stones with holes in them. Don't have chalk where you live? Just use normal stones, as I did with the flint.

2 To make the stone handles, cut a 16in (40cm) length of rattan cord or twine (I used twine salvaged from the footstool project on page 18). Heat up the glue gun and apply a line of glue around the center of the stone.

3 Wrap the cord twice around the stone, keeping the unused ends even. Add more glue as necessary to keep the cord in place.

4 Make your other handles in the same way. Don't trim the ends of the cord as these are what you use to attach the handles to the drawer.

5 To make the chalk handles, cut a 12 in (30cm) length of cord and simply thread it through the holes, pulling it tight and keeping the ends an even length.

6 Mark where you want the handles to go on the drawer fronts, measuring them to make sure they are level.

7 Drill two holes ¾ in (2cm) from each other. Repeat on the other side of the drawer front.

8 Push the long lengths of cord through the holes and tie them together on the inside of the drawer with a triple knot. Trim the ends of the cord.

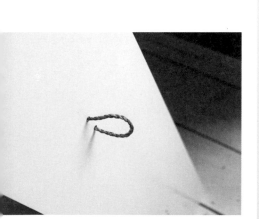

9 To make the cord handles, drill the holes in the same way. Push a length of cord through the holes, leaving a loop of 2 in (5cm) on the outside of the drawer. Tie in place with a triple knot, as in step 8.

INSTANT UPDATE

Bedside light

This bedside light will add a real pop of color to your bedroom and it's made within 5 minutes! The bare bulb of this minimalist light brings a great industrial look to the room. Colored power cords are making a real comeback and this vintage fabric cable is easily available to purchase online (see page 110). The light cord hangs from a wooden bracket previously used to support a shelf. You might have one left over from a recent shelving project, or you can purchase them very cheaply in home improvement and do-it-yourself stores.

YOU WILL NEED

- colored electrical cord with light fitting and plug
- pencil
- drill
- wall plugs and screws
- wooden bracket
- screwdriver
- light bulb

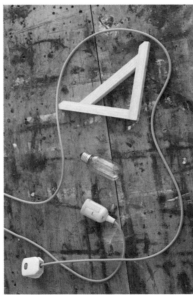

1 It is possible to buy the electrical cord with the light fitting and plug attached online. However, if you purchase all the items separately, ask an electrician to wire them together for you.

TIP
The light bulb does get hot so, as it doesn't have a shade around it, this light shouldn't be used in children's rooms.

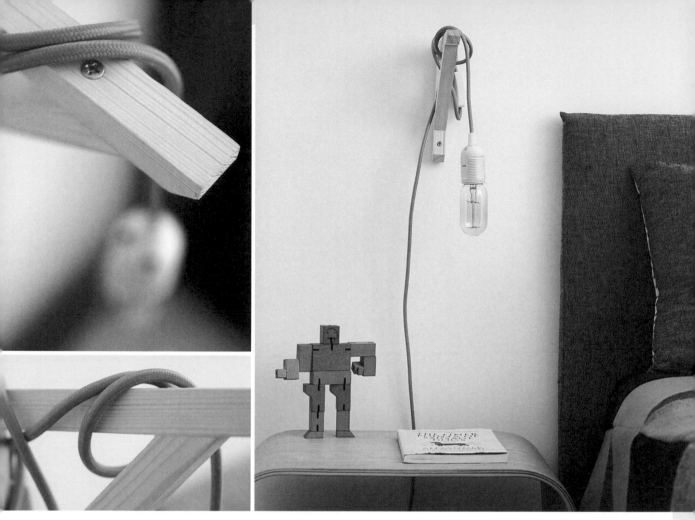

2 Decide where you want your light to go on the wall. Mark the two holes you need to drill by sticking a pencil through the hole and marking the wall. Drill the two holes (see page 106), insert the wall plugs, and attach the bracket with screws.

3 Screw the bulb into its fitting. There are a wide variety of bulbs on the market in an even bigger price range. Pick one that suits the style of your room and has the right wattage for the fitting.

4 Wrap the cord around the bracket so it looks pretty and is secure, and that's it—your light is finished!

WINDOW SHUTTERS

I am seriously obsessed with shutters! I'd been thinking of making my own but never could work out an easy way to do so, until I looked at one of my old wooden Venetian window shades. I realized it would make a great shutter, as the thin wooden slats are easy to weave. To bring a ski-lodge feel to my guest room I didn't make the shutter full length, so the light comes in through the top part of the window. You can make the shutters the full height of the window if you prefer, or hang a blackout shade behind the shutter if you are a very light sleeper.

YOU WILL NEED

- slatted wooden Venetian shade
- scissors
- measuring rule
- ¾ x 1½ in (2 x 4cm) wood—length depends on the dimension of your window
- saw
- drill
- small wood screws
- screwdriver
- masking tape
- wood stain or paint
- paintbrush
- four hinges
- strong glue

1 Find an old Venetian shade wide enough to make a decent-sized shutter. Cut the cords between the slats and separate all the slats.

2 I made my shutters the height of the slats (this saves you a lot of sawing). Measure your window and calculate how wide and high your shutters need to be. Each shutter frame will need two long uprights and two horizontal bars. Cut your wood to size.

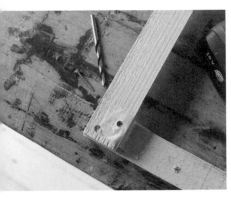

3 Predrill two holes at each end of the long uprights. Position the holes on the diagonal, as this reduces the chance of the wood splitting. Place the drilled upright on top of the horizontal bar, align the corners, and screw the pieces together. It can help to hold the frame in place with masking tape.

4 Screw together the remaining three corners. Make the second frame in the same way.

5 Lay the slats vertically on the frame, with the ends resting on the upper and lower parts of the frame. Predrill a hole in the top and bottom of each slat, positioning the holes centrally in each slat to avoid splitting the slat. If you try to put a screw through the slat without pre-drilling, the wood of the slat will split.

6 Screw the slats into the top and bottom of the frame using small wood screws.

7 Cut 16 slats the width of the shutter frame.

8 Take four of the slats and weave them between the long vertical slats. This will give more stability to the shutter and also hide some of the little holes in the slats. Weave them in by moving the small slats under and then over the long slats. Make sure you alternate, so if you started the first one by going under, start the second short slat by going over.

9 Make sure that the short slats are evenly spaced. Fix their ends into the frame by predrilling a hole and then screwing in place with a wood screw.

10 Your shutter should now look like this. Construct the second shutter in the same way.

11 Stain the frame the same color as the slats and allow to dry. Apply a second coat if necessary. I used a dark stain for my shutters.

12 Attach two hinges per shutter, placing them on the front of the shutter 6 in (15cm) from the top and bottom of the frame. Make sure you screw them on so that the hinge opens the right way.

13 Fix the shutters to the window frame by screwing the hinge to the frame.

14 The remaining eight short slats are used to cover the screws in the frame. Apply a small amount of glue to the top and bottom of the vertical part of the frame, then stick the slats in place. If you wish, you could also glue another vertical slat to each side of the shutter, to cover up the screws holding the horizontal slats in place.

UNDER-BED STORAGE

This project upcycles drawers from a bedside unit into neat under-bed storage. You might be lucky and find one large drawer that fits beneath your bed perfectly—I didn't, so instead I used two small drawers. The only downside is the dust that can accumulate under the bed, but topping the drawer with an old roller shade keeps the contents dust-free. A patterned self-adhesive vinyl gives a new look to the drawers—this comes in all sorts of designs, including the graphic paint splatters used here.

YOU WILL NEED

- two old drawers
- saw
- three metal repair plates
- screws and screwdriver
- offcuts of wood
- wood glue
- four small caster wheels
- self-adhesive vinyl
- measuring rule
- scissors
- old credit or store card
- old roller shade
- needle and thick thread

1 Find two drawers that fit underneath your bed. When measuring their dimensions, bear in mind that the drawers will have extra height once the caster wheels are attached.

2 The drawers I used have a wide front but, as I didn't like having a big gap in the middle, I cut off a slice of the wooden fascia to make them sit close together.

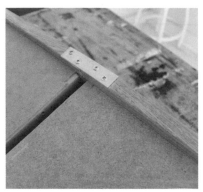

3 Use repair plates to connect your drawers together. Screw two of them in place on the back of the drawers—behind the front piece of wood and on the back of the drawers.

4 Screw the third repair plate on the base of the drawer fronts.

5 The base of the drawers will be too thin to screw the caster wheels into, so use small offcuts of wood to give the drawer base more depth. Glue these in place in the four outer corners of your drawers.

TIP
I used two swivel wheels and two fixed wheels because that's what I had to hand. If using fixed wheels, make sure you attach them in the correct direction so they move forward, rather than sideways.

6 Screw the wheels in place on the underside of the drawers. The screws will also keep the wooden blocks in place.

7 To give the drawers a more uniform look and to disguise the join between the drawers, use a self-adhesive vinyl. Measure the drawer front, allowing extra for the vinyl to wrap around the edges, and cut the vinyl to these dimensions. It's very easy to cut in straight lines as most vinyl backing papers are printed with a grid.

  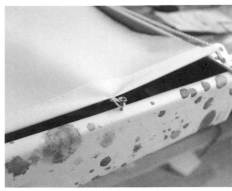

8 Stick the vinyl on little by little and smooth it down with the credit card, making sure you push out any air bubbles trapped underneath the vinyl. Wrap the vinyl neatly around the corners, clipping into the vinyl a little as necessary. Cover the sides in the same way.

9 Find a roller shade that is the same width as the drawer or use one that you can cut down to size. Follow the manufacturer's instructions for attaching the brackets that hold the shade to one end of the drawer.

10 Most roller shades come with a safety hook for the pull cord. Screw this into the edge of the drawer at the opposite end to the brackets to keep the blind pulled taut. Stitch a little loop on the lower edge of the shade and screw a small wood screw to the side of the drawer to act as a fastener and keep the covering in place.

 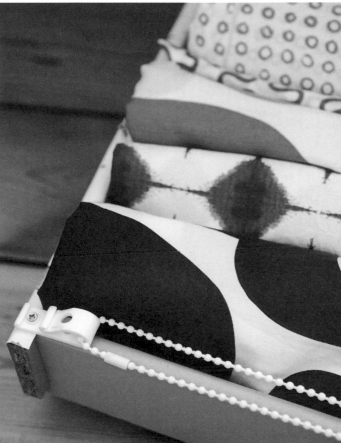

CHAPTER 4
HOME OFFICE

BOOKCASE SIDEBOARD

Is your home in need of some sophisticated storage? If so, try making this sideboard. It has plenty of space for storing paperwork and provides a great surface for displaying artworks or trinkets. The sideboard began life as an upright bookcase and had been in my home from the moment I came to live in the U.K. years ago. It originally belonged to a friend and moved house with us three times. The bookcase then continued its travels with me to a further three homes, so the time had come for a makeover!

YOU WILL NEED

- bookcase
- masking tape
- drill
- spare wood or MDF (medium-density fiberboard)
- measuring rule
- saw
- corner brackets (four per shelf)
- screws
- screwdriver
- four small wooden table legs, approximately 3¼ in (8cm) tall
- filler
- sandpaper
- paint
- paintbrush

1 Remove the shelves from the bookcase. These probably sit on little metal plugs which makes removing them easy. One of the middle shelves was screwed in and I decided to leave it there as it was in a good position, but unscrew if you want to change the spacing of your shelves.

TIP

If you already know what you want to store where, measure large items so that the storage spaces in the sideboard will be the perfect size.

2 Turn the bookcase on its side and decide where you want the vertical spacers to go. The spacers are made from the shelves you have removed as they are already the exact fit. I created three spacers in my sideboard. Also consider where you want to add horizontal shelves and make sure they fit between the spacers. My original bookcase had four shelves—I used three as spacers and one as a shelf. The two additional shelves are made from leftover pieces of MDF.

3 Drill holes for the screws that will hold the vertical spacers in place. I stuck a strip of masking tape to the side of the bookcase to make sure the holes are in a straight line. Drill two holes on each side of the bookcase for each spacer, then screw the spacers in place.

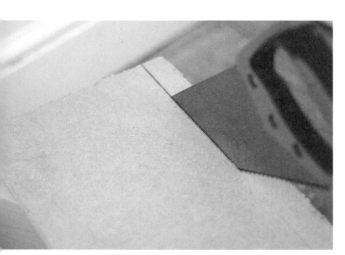

4 Cut your shelves from leftover wood or MDF. Two of my shelves are the same depth as the bookcase, but I made one central shelf less deep to give the sideboard a more informal look.

5 Use four corner brackets per shelf to attach your shelves to the spacers. Screw the brackets to the underside of the shelves first, then slot the shelves in place and screw to the spacers.

6 Decide where to place the legs, then drill the holes and attach in place. Make sure you measure and position them accurately as you don't want your sideboard to wobble.

7 Fill any holes from the original bookcase or any new screw holes that are visible with filler. When the filler has dried, smooth it down with sandpaper.

8 Paint the sideboard all over, inside and out. I used a soft gray. You will probably need to apply two coats of paint to get an even finish—allow to dry thoroughly between coats.

9 Add some accent colors on your sideboard. I gave the legs, little shelf, and the original bookcase base a coat of bright yellow paint (you may need to apply two coats). The color really pops against the gray and makes the sideboard look more modern.

INSTANT UPDATE

Bulletin board

This is a very quick hack—you will only need a couple of minutes to give a boring noticeboard a new look. Using just a small length of fabric, you can match the look of your board to the décor of your office. I've used a sturdy cotton fabric, as this will withstand the pins being pushed in. You can opt for a bold pattern, like this chevron print, or go for something more delicate, such as a flower print. Or take the upcycling element a stage further and use old jeans to cover your board.

YOU WILL NEED
- cork bulletin board
- fabric
- scissors
- staple gun

1 Choose a piece of fabric large enough to cover your board and wrap around to the reverse side. Lay the fabric on a flat surface, wrong side facing up. Place the board on top of the fabric and cut around it, allowing a minimum of 2 in (5cm) on each side.

2 Fold the fabric of the short sides over to the reverse side of the board and staple in place. Make sure you pull the fabric tight before stapling.

3 Fold the fabric over the longer sides and staple in place, working from the center out toward the corners.

4 To make neat corners, fold the corner diagonally, then tuck over the other sides—it's a bit like wrapping a present.

5 When your corner looks nice and neat, staple the fabric in place. Turn the board over and it is ready to be used.

GRAPHIC FILING CABINET

Filing cabinets are undoubtedly extremely useful, but they are just so ugly—large metal beasts in drab colors that take up lots of space in your office. Wouldn't it be fun to disguise them as a graphic piece of furniture instead? So, with a lick of paint, some sheets of wrapping paper, and a piece of wood leftover from another project, I managed to give mine a proper makeover. My filing cabinet was originally an inexpensive purchase from a local junk yard, but you wouldn't guess that looking at it now!

YOU WILL NEED

- old filing cabinet
- masking tape
- paint and paintbrush
- leftover piece of wood
- measuring rule
- saw
- strong glue, such as No More Nails
- electric sander
- wrapping paper
- varnish glue
- craft knife
- chalkboard label
- washi tape

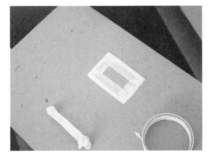

1 Clean your filing cabinet so it is free from dust and grime. Use masking tape to cover the handles, lock, and label holders to protect them against paint splatters.

2 I used bright blue milk paint on my cabinet. Most paints will stick to metal, but test the paint will adhere by painting a small area on the back of the cabinet first. Let the paint dry and, if necessary, apply another coat.

3 I used small pieces of weathered outdoor planks of wood on top of my cabinet, but one solid block would work equally well. If using small pieces, measure and cut them to size, creating a jigsaw puzzle effect on the top. Alternatively, measure and cut one piece of wood to size.

4 Use strong glue to attach the wood to the metal top. Apply the glue to the cabinet and place the wood in position, butting the pieces closely together. Weigh the wood down with stacks of heavy books to make sure it sticks to the cabinet properly, then leave the glue to set.

5 When the glue has dried, use a sander to smooth down the wood. Pay particular attention to the edges, as they need to be rounded and smooth.

6 I decorated the drawer fronts by covering them in wrapping paper. Give the drawer a coat of varnish glue and stick the paper on, pressing it down evenly and smoothing out any air bubbles. Use a craft knife to cut away the paper around the label holder.

7 To get the paper to lie smoothly around the handle, make two cuts in the paper from the bottom edge to the handle, then fold and smooth the paper under and around the handle, trimming it where necessary.

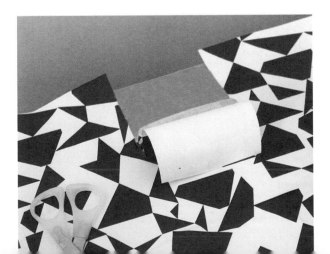

8 Seal the paper with a top coat of varnish glue and allow to dry thoroughly.

9 Stick chalkboard labels on the label holders. Decorate the label holders with washi tape.

TIP

I'm using one of the cabinet drawers for files and the other one for my fabrics. A filing cabinet is a very neat way to store your fabric stash—simply cut the filing folders in half and hang your fabrics over the metal hanging strip. This will put an end to tumbling stacks of fabrics.

OFFICE TABLE UPDATE

Sometimes you have a piece of furniture that has seen better days but you just can't get rid of it, like my desk. I have had this table since the age of 19, when I moved out of my parents' house. The table started life as my work desk/table/ storage spot in my student digs. It later became my dining-room table, and then served as my sewing table. I still love its shape and the matching chairs are extremely comfy, so I decided to give it a facelift and now I use it in my office. A lick of paint and some washi tape are all you need.

YOU WILL NEED

- old table in need of an update
- paint
- foam paintbrushes
- masking tape
- old cloths
- washi tape
- clear varnish

1 Make sure your table is clean and dust free. I started by painting the side edges of my table bright blue. I like using foam brushes, as they drip less and you can cover the side of the table in one smooth move.

2 Next, paint the table legs. If your table is similar to mine and has metal bits you want to keep unpainted, cover them with masking tape. Place little bits of cloth underneath the table legs to protect the floor from paint drips. If you are really messy, you might want to use a full-size dust sheet.

3 I wanted to keep some of the tabletop wood on show so I used masking tape to make two stripes, one a little wider than the other. As the table legs and sides have been painted a bright color, I decided to keep the top of the table very clean by painting it a bright white.

4 When the paint is almost dry, carefully peel away the masking tape to reveal your stripes. To add more decorative detail to the tabletop, apply four stripes of washi tape, sticking them along the edges of the white lines (this will also cover any slightly smudged paint lines).

5 Give the whole table a coat of varnish. This will protect the painted surfaces and seal in the washi tape. Allow the varnish to dry thoroughly before using the table.

CHAPTER 5

OUTDOOR SPACE

APPLE CRATE TABLE

Add some rustic charm to your seating area by making an outdoor coffee table from an old wooden apple crate. Look in vintage markets or brocante stores for a suitable crate, or you could even ask at a local orchard! Other wooden crates with similar dimensions would work just as well. If you wish, add a piece of glass, cut to size, to the top for a more sophisticated finish.

YOU WILL NEED

- old apple crate, or similar wooden crate
- wooden poles for the legs (choose wood pretreated for outdoor use)
- saw
- sandpaper
- drill
- wood glue
- masking tape
- long screws
- screwdriver
- paint suitable for outdoor use
- paintbrush

1 Decide how high you would like your table to be—mine is 12 in (30cm). Using the saw, cut the wooden poles into four pieces of that length. Sand the cut edges to smooth them down.

2 Drill two holes at each corner of the crate, at the points where you wish to attach the table legs. I have drilled through the side of the crate, so the screws will not appear on the tabletop. If you drill the two holes in a diagonal line, there is less chance of the wood splitting.

3 Apply wood glue to the top of each leg and press the legs into position.

4 To make it easier to keep the legs in place, wrap a length of masking tape around the crate and each leg. Screw each leg to the crate, using screws that are long enough to go through the crate and into each leg. Remove the masking tape.

5 You can choose to keep your table the way it is or give it a lick of paint. I decided to whitewash mine, so you can still see the original printing on the apple crate. Make a whitewash by adding a splash of water to the paint—the more water you add, the thinner the paint will be (see page 108). Apply with a paintbrush and leave to dry.

SHOWER CURTAIN CANOPY

The moment the weather is good enough to sit outside I'm there, even if this means wrapping myself up in a blanket to combat chilly evenings. There is just something so relaxing about sitting outside. To make my lounging corner even cozier, I added a canopy. It provides shade in the height of summer, and helps to retain the warmth when the weather isn't so great. This canopy is super easy to make as it uses an old shower curtain. I chose one with a great print, but you could go monochrome if you prefer.

YOU WILL NEED

- shower curtain
- scissors
- measuring tape
- pins
- thread
- sewing machine
- fence post
- saw
- chisel
- sandpaper
- flat metal repair plates
- screws
- screwdriver
- long wooden pole or batten
- paint and paintbrush
- binding twine
- nylon rope

MAKING THE CANOPY

1 Lay your shower curtain flat on the floor and cut it into a triangle. My curtain was square, measuring 70 x 70 in (180 x 180cm), so I just cut it diagonally from one corner to the other. Use the triangle without the top strip of grommet holes for the main canopy.

2 From the other triangle, cut off the strip that has the grommets in it. Cut this into three pieces—you will need two lengths of 4 in (10cm) and one long strip.

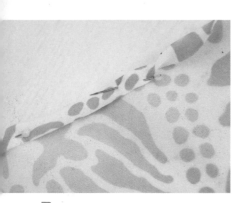

3 Make a rolled hem on the long unhemmed side of your curtain. You do this by folding over ½ in (1cm) of the edge and then folding it over again. Pin and machine stitch in place.

4 Find the middle of the curtain by folding the triangle in half along the long side. Pin the long strip of grommets to this central fold line on the right side of the fabric. Allow 4 in (10cm) of the grommet strip to overhang at both corners. Machine stitch down both sides of the grommet strip. Strengthen the ends by stitching over them a couple of times—these are the hanging points so will need to take the tension.

5 Pin the two shorter grommet strips to the other two corners of the canopy and stitch in place, again making sure they are attached securely.

CONSTRUCTING THE SUPPORT FRAME

Now you have your canopy ready, it's time to start the frame construction. You need one long pole in front of your canopy and three points to tie the corners to. The easiest way is to drill three hooks into a garden fence or wall, but here I'm going to show you how you can attach the canopy if it's not possible to drill holes. The instructions for making this bench are on page 99, but you could use any sturdy wooden bench.

6 Start by attaching a fence post to the back of your bench. You will need to remove a notch from the post so that it sits neatly around your bench. Do this by measuring the width of the back of the bench and saw it to the right depth. With a chisel, cut out the required bit of wood (see page 102) and sand to remove any rough edges.

7 Attach the post to your bench by screwing a flat metal repair plate on both sides of the post.

8 Take the long pole that will sit in front of the bench and paint it whatever color you like. When the paint was dry, I wrapped the pole in twine—this was just to add some decorative texture, but local cats might view it as a giant scratching post!

9 Place the pole in front of your bench (ask a friend to hold it or prop it up with chairs, as seen here). Attach a long piece of nylon rope to the top of the pole by wrapping it around the pole several times and tying tightly, then run it to a point at the same height opposite of the pole—in my case, a hook for the laundry line. You can use any strong point, like a screw or a tree branch, or tie it to a fence. Don't put too much tension on the rope just yet (you will do that in step 12).

10 Attach long lengths of twine to the grommets in the three corners of your canopy and to the grommet in the center of the long side.

11 Attach a screw or hook to the bench fence post at the required height of your canopy and tie the apex hanging point to this. If your shower curtain is paterned, make sure the pattern faces down.

12 Now tie the canopy's central point on the long side to the tall pole, run twine through the ring twice (for extra strength), and tie it securely to the pole. Once the canopy is attached to both the back and front points, you can tighten the nylon rope attached to the long pole to ensure the pole stands upright.

13 Tie the corner points to nearby branches, walls, fences, or screws. The two outer corners should be a little lower than the front and back of the canopy to create a tent shape.

14 Make sure there is enough tension on the canopy so that any rain will drain off the tent, rather than create puddles on the fabric as this could break your canopy. All you need to do now is sit back and enjoy your new nomad-style seating corner.

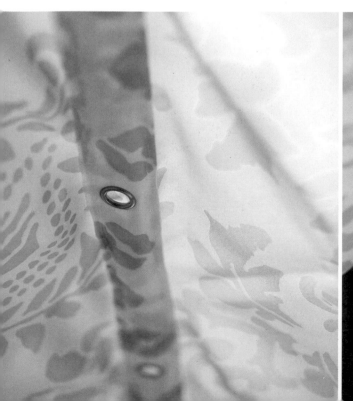

OUTDOOR BENCH

Do you have some decking boards left over from a previous garden project? If so, why not turn them into an outdoor sofa? This L-shaped corner bench provides great seating if you have lots of friends over, and can be made in a day. It's also perfect for smaller gardens as it doesn't take up too much space. One side of this bench measures 60 in (152cm), the other measures 54 in (138cm), and it is 16 in (42cm) deep, but you can alter the dimensions to suit either your garden or your supply of wood.

YOU WILL NEED

- five 2 x 2 in (5 x 5cm) fence posts, 69 in (175cm) high
- measuring rule
- saw
- sandpaper
- drill

- wood screws
- electric screwdriver
- eight 71 in (180cm) lengths of 1½ x ¾ in (4 x 2cm) outdoor wood
- four decking boards, 6 in (15cm) wide

- two 71 in (180cm) lengths of 4 x ¾ in (10 x 2cm) outdoor wood
- six corner brackets
- outdoor wood paint
- paintbrush

MAKING THE BASIC FRAME

1 Saw one of the fence posts into three pieces, measuring 37 in (94cm) for the rear upright, 15½ in (39cm) for the front upright, and 16½ in (42cm) for the seat support. These will form the stands for the decking boards to rest on. Sand the rough edges away.

2 To attach the 16½ in (42cm) seat piece on top of the 15½ in (39cm) front upright, mark where they join and drill two holes through one end of the seat support. Make sure the holes are diagonal rather than opposite each other, as this will reduce the risk of the wood splitting. Join them together with two wood screws.

3 Now fix the joined seat and front upright to the rear upright. Screw a corner bracket to the underside of the seat support and fix this to the rear upright. To ensure your stand does not wobble, make sure the bottoms of the uprights are level. You now have one stand, so repeat this process with the remaining four fence posts to make a total of five stands.

4 To add more stability to the stands, add a support piece between the front and rear uprights. Saw five 18½ in (47cm) support pieces from the 1½ x ¾ in (4 x 2cm) wood. Drill holes and screw them to the stands, positioning them 2 in (5cm) from the bottom. Make sure the two stands that will meet in the corner have the supports fixed on the inside as this looks nicer and makes it easier to join the two corner pieces together later.

MAKING THE SEATING

5 Saw the decking boards into three pieces 35½ in (90cm) long and another three pieces 71 in (180cm) long. It is easier to cut the wood on the smooth side, rather than on the ridged side.

6 Line up three of the stands (it may help to prop them up with chairs) and attach the longer decking boards to the stands with wood screws.

7 Fix the decking to each stand using six wood screws per plank. Line up the two remaining stands and attach the shorter decking boards in the same way. You will now have two freestanding benches.

ADDING THE BACK REST

8 Push the two benches together to create an L-shape. The backrest wood will eventually hold the bench together, but for extra stability attach a corner bracket on the back where the backrest post of the short bench meets the seating post of the long bench.

9 From the 1½ x ¾ in (4 x 2cm) wood, saw three pieces 71 in (180cm) long and three pieces 55 in (140cm) long. Drilling holes and using wood screws, attach the first long piece at the top of the post and the other two pieces below, with 2 in (5cm) gaps in between.

10 For the shorter bench, the back rest needs to be fixed behind the corner fence post of the longer bench but in front of the post on the right-hand side. Screw the timber in place with 2 in (5cm) gaps in between.

FINISHING OFF

11 To make sure your seating cushions do not slide off the back of the bench, make a little ledge. Using the 1½ x ¾ in (4 x 2cm) wood, saw one 71 in (180cm) length and one 55 in (140cm) length. Attach with one wood screw per post.

12 Finish the bench by adding the 4 x ¾ in (10 x 2cm) wood to the top of the fence-post stands. This secures the bench, covers the open wood ends, and creates a great mini shelf for glasses or candles. Saw one 71 in (180cm) length and one 55 in (140cm) length and screw to the posts.

13 Finally, protect the bench with outdoor wood paint so that it can stay outside all year round. You will probably need to apply two or three coats, depending on the color you use. I painted my bench a stone color, which is not quite as bright as pure white.

TOOLS AND TECHNIQUES

Here is a guide to the tools and materials I have found to be really useful. You don't need to buy them all at once, especially if you start with some of the simpler projects or instant updates. There are a few techniques you'll need to get the hang of, and I've explained those here, too.

WOODWORKING AND DIY

These are the tools I like to use, followed by step-by-step instructions on how to use them. I have also talked about different types of wood and fasteners.

GENERAL TOOLS

Handsaw (1) Use for straight cuts and for thick planks or poles. I like using a handsaw, as it doesn't need a power supply so is very portable. See also page 104.

Junior hacksaw (2) For hand-sawing curved shapes in thin wood. Also good for cutting thin metals, like pipes.

Miter box Made from plastic or wood, these make precise miter cuts at 45- and 90-degree angles. Cutting two pieces of wood with a 45-degree angle means you can join them to create a 90-degree corner. I use mine with a **backsaw (3)**, but you could equally use a miter saw. See also page 104.

Screwdrivers (4) It's handy to have both types of screwdrivers in several different sizes:

• Flat head—for slot screws, also great for opening paint cans and taking out old staples and nails.

• Phillips head—for use on crosshead screws.

Hammers (5) I use a smaller, lighter hammer for small nails and a heavier one to hammer in big nails. It's also handy to have a claw hammer, as the claw pulls nails out of walls and pieces of wood.

Sandpaper (6) For smaller pieces of wood and hard-to-reach places, it's easier to use sandpaper than the palm sander. It comes in different grades of coarseness:

• Coarse grid 40–60 for heavy sanding and stripping

• Medium grid 80–120 for smoothing surfaces and small imperfections

• Extra fine grid 360–600 for finishing surfaces and smoothing

It comes in sanding pads and as sandpaper. I like to use a sanding block—a piece of cork that you wrap in sandpaper, which gives more grip when sanding longer pieces. For sanding small places, roll the paper up until it fits the space. Use a dust tack cloth—this will remove all sanding dust before painting.

Corner square (7) Use a corner square to check your angles—for example, when putting up shelves, hold the corner in place to ensure you have a 90-degree angle. I use an 8 x 12 in (20 x 30cm) metal square.

Chisel (8) Used to cut out a groove or channel of wood for joints (as in the garden canopy on page 93).

Mark the position and depth of the groove and use a handsaw to cut both edges. Make sure you don't go deeper than your mark. When you have made the saw cuts, use the chisel to cut the rest of the wood out. The chisel has a metal top that you hit with a hammer—this will make the chisel gouge out the wood little by little until you have the cut you need.

C clamp (9) Keeps your project in place when sawing or gluing.

Staple gun I love this as it's a quick and easy way to attach fabric to a wood frame, as in the wallpaper canvas on page 12, or to upholster a chair, as on page 41.

To use, put your fabric in place and hold your staple gun flat on the fabric, press the trigger to release the staple into the fabric. If the fabric is thick or the wood very strong, you might need to use your other hand to push down the stapler to make sure the staple goes through all the materials.

Filler (10) Filler is great for hiding drill holes in wood and damages in your wall or for masking screws. I prefer using quick-drying filler. To use, push the filler into the hole using a putty knife. Scrap the knife over the surface

to make it as flat as possible. When dried, sand down the excess filler and your surface is ready to paint.

Glue (11) For the projects in this book I use wood glue, epoxy glue, and a super strong glue, like No More Nails.

You will also need:

- Measuring rule (12)
- Spirit level (13)
- Masking tape (14)
- Stanley knife (15)
- Scraper (16)
- Pliers (17)
- Pencil

WOOD

Outdoor wood Suitable for garden projects, this is treated to help prolong its life and protect against rot or insect attack. This soft wood has a green or brown color to it, depending which preservative has been used.

Decking boards Usually laid as decking in your backyard, I used it to make an outdoor sofa, page 98.

Softwood Mainly pine or spruce, used in a huge range of general indoor projects. It's cheap and very easy to work with. Comes in sawn, which is rough and normally used when you don't see the wood, or planed, like the wood used in my projects which has smooth surface.

MDF (medium-density fiberboard) Made from powdered wood that has been pressed together with glue to form a sheet. I love working with this as it is easy to cut and sand and

looks great with a paint finish as it's so smooth. MDF comes in different thicknesses, so use a thicker sheet if your build needs to carry weight. Always use a dust mask suitable for use with MDF when sawing/sanding. Alternatively, most home improvement or DIY stores will cut MDF sheets to size for you, which saves you a lot of work. MDF soaks up water like a sponge, so don't use in a wet place or outdoors, and don't use diluted paints on it.

Driftwood Pieces of wood that have been washed ashore. This wood is brittle but comes in great shapes (as in the kitchen door handles on page 36).

Wood offcuts I love using leftover pieces of wood for my projects—have a look first at what you have left in your garage or shed before buying new wood.

POWER TOOLS

Jigsaw (1) Great for cutting shapes in wood up to 2½ in (6.5cm) thick.

Cordless combi drill (2) Multi-tool for drilling holes and screwing in screws, works on a battery so easy to use anywhere in the house or garden. Use the right drill bit for your project. For the projects in this book you need wood, masonry, and tile drill bits **(4)**.

Palm sander (3) Small and light and fits in one hand. Use the right grade of sanding pad for your projects. Align the Velcro pads with the ventilation holes. You can attach the sander to your vacuum cleaner or use its dust pouch to catch all the sanding dust.

Saw bits (4) Use the correct saw bit in your jigsaw—metal and wood require different saw bits.

Power Tool Health and Safety

- Always wear the appropriate safety clothing and accessories.
- Never wear loose clothing that can get caught up in machinery.
- Keep long hair tied up.
- Check your power tool before plugging it into the mains. Make sure that the electric cable is intact and has no bare wires, that any blades are secure, and that sanding pads are secured properly in place.
- Tuck wire cables away from where you are working.
- Always switch off power tools at the source before adjusting settings or changing drill or saw bits.
- Always follow the manufacturer's instructions.

FASTENERS

Multipurpose screws (1) With a sharp point to drive through the wood, these are designed for use on a variety of materials, such as hardwood, chipboard, and MDF, without the need for predrilling. Keep a selection of different lengths in your toolbox. Screws with a golden hue are zinc-plated ones; they have better corrosion resistance, so are great for outdoor use.

Hook screws and picture hangers (2) Hook screws and screw eyes have a hooped end, which makes them ideal for hanging things on a batten. Picture hooks are great for hanging artwork.

Wall plugs and screws (3) Use in interior and exterior walls to hold screws in place. Check walls for pipes or power cables before drilling a hole (see page 106).

Nuts and bolts (4) Used together when the bolt runs all the way through the wood and is secured on the other end with a nut or cap.

Nails (5) Wire nails are used for general work, but they can split wood.

Panel pins (6) Lightweight and a popular way of joining wood, although glue is usually used as part of the join. They are thin, so there is less chance of splitting wood.

Corner brackets (7) I love using these to join timber at right angles—easy and quick to use.

Repair plate (8) Used to repair wood or, in my case, to attach two drawers together (see page 72).

Upholstery tags (9) Use these tags to finish your upholstery projects.

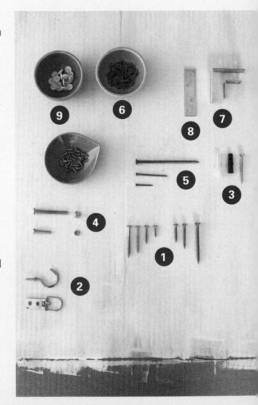

TECHNIQUES

Using a handsaw Mark the cutting line, then make a starting cut just outside the marked line. Cut next to your cutting line, as you lose a very tiny amount of wood to sawdust and you don't want your wood to end up a little short.

You can use your thumb or knuckle as a guide for the blade to ensure your saw stays on the right spot. I don't like to have my hands anywhere near a sharp blade, so I start off making very small saw movements until I have a notch in which the saw blade fits nicely. Then you can start making bigger strokes, keeping your saw at a 45-degree angle. Don't press on the saw—let the blade do the hard work.

Sawing a miter cut Measure your wood accurately and draw a cutting line. One side of the wood will be longer—to keep track of which side will be which and to measure correctly, always measure the long side of the 45-degree cut.

1 Place the wood in the miter box—small pieces are easier to keep in place with clamps, while longer pieces can be held.

2 Start sawing with light pressure to score the cutting line, then increase the pressure to cut the wood. The miter box will guide your cut, but keep your saw straight.

Using a jigsaw Make sure you have a stable surface to saw on— a work bench, table, or Workmate, like the one I use here. Remember that the wood being cut should overhang your worksurface.

1 Fit the jigsaw with the correct blade for the material you wish to saw.

2 Draw a cutting line on the wood. Press the saw firmly on the wood with the blade away from the edge. Start the motor and guide the blade outside the cutting line—a little wood will get lost in sawdust so cut just next to the line and your measurements will still be correct. Move the saw forward at a pace that allows the blade to cut the wood without deflecting—don't try to push the saw forward. Switch off the saw before moving it away from the wood.

3 Jigsaws are great to use on curved shapes or to saw out shapes in the center of wood, like handles. For this, you need to drill a hole in the middle of your shape, insert the blade, and gently guide the saw along the cutting line.

Predrilling wood Also called making a pilot hole, this will prevent smaller or thinner pieces of wood splitting when you screw in a wood screw. It also helps you to drive the screw in straight when working with denser hard woods.

1 Mark the spot where you need to drill. Choose the correct size of wood drill bit—you need a bit slightly smaller than the diameter of your screw, as you need to retain enough wood for the screw threads to grip. If in doubt, opt for the smaller drill bit.

2 Drill your pilot hole to a depth equal to the screw's length, making sure you keep your drill at the angle you want your screw to go.

Predrilling is also used when you want to hide screw heads (as in the two-chair bench on page 34). Choose a drill bit the same size as, or slightly bigger, than the screw heads you use. Drill the hole halfway through the wood and when you screw in your screw, it will completely disappear. Once the screw is fixed, you can fill the leftover hole with filler (see page 102).

Drilling a hole in a wall Always check walls for pipes and power cables before drilling a hole. Choose the right wall plug and screw for what you need to hang. Use a masonry drill bit the same width as your wall plug. Hold the wall plug next to your drill bit and, with a bit of tape, mark how long your plug is—this is how deep you need to drill.

1 Drill the hole, making sure you keep the drill straight. Insert the wall plug and hammer in place.

2 Screw in your screw and hang whatever you want to hang.

Using a palm sander
This is great for furniture or large projects, and much faster than using sandpaper.

1 Choose the right grid pad and attach under your sander, making sure the exhaust holes match up.

2 Press down firmly on your wood and switch on. Move the sander back and forth across the grain. Don't apply too much pressure—let the pad do the work.

PAINT AND WALLPAPER

Painting a piece of furniture is a really quick way to give it a whole new character. Wallpaper can be a great material to use, too.

MATERIALS AND TOOLS

Interior paint Indoor paints are either water- or oil-based. Oil paints are durable but can take a very long time to dry. Gloss is a common oil paint and gives a great long-lasting shine to wood. Water-based paints, like latex or emulsion, are becoming more hardwearing, plus they dry quickly and are far less smelly then gloss paint. Water-based paint is available in matte, satin (soft sheen), and silk (high sheen) finishes. For most furniture projects in this book I used milk paint (I like the General Finishes brand). A modern version of traditional paint with a strong mineral base, it is easy to use and you can mix, lighten, and distress it.

Multipurpose decorative paint This paint is matte, fast drying, and sticks to nearly any surface without requiring any preparation, like sanding or priming. I like using Annie Sloan's Chalk Paint® brand.

Exterior paint Use this special blended paint for outdoor projects as it is designed to withstand sun, wind, water, and mildew.

Varnish This top coat for your paintwork will make it last longer. Gloss or satin varnishes give an attractive shine. Some varnishes contain a UV stabilizer to prevent it breaking down in sunlight and to protect the underlying stain or paint from fading. Apply your varnish the same way as paint when the final coat of paint is completely dry.

Paintbrushes Foam brushes are great for small projects and for pieces with hard-to-reach areas. They do not leave brush strokes and are great for retouching paintwork, but can only be washed a couple of times. Bristle brushes are more expensive, but you can clean (see page 108) and use them over and over again. Bristle brushes do show brush strokes, so they can add some texture to your paintwork. They are great for big projects.

Drop cloth This protects your floor from paint drips. I use an old curtain but you can buy plastic sheets.

Masking tape Used for taping over areas you don't want to paint. This could be the baseboard/skirting board when painting a wall or parts of a desk you don't want painted (as on page 86). Stick the tape over areas not to be painted and press the edges down well. Paint your item, painting over the tape. When the paint is still a little wet, carefully peel off the tape.

Wallpaper It's not just to decorate your walls! This can be used to cover doors and to make paintings as well. There are some great patterns available.

Containers for paint and glue When mixing paint, glue, or paste, I use throwaway containers as this saves a lot of cleaning. Paper cups are useful for small amounts of paint, paper plates are good when mixing glue, and the bottom of a milk carton provides a great container for wallpaper paste and water-diluted paints.

You will also need:
- Paint stirrers
- Wiping cloths

TECHNIQUES

How to paint

1 Paint must be stirred before use as heavier ingredients sink to the bottom. Use a paint stirrer, a small piece of wood, or an old wooden spoon to give it a good mix.

2 Dip the lower third of the foam brush or bristle brush in the paint. Let the excess drip off or lightly scrape it on the edge of the paint can.

3 Apply the paint to your surface in long, smooth strokes until the paint begins to thin, then reload the brush with paint and repeat.

4 Your project will probably need more than one coat of paint. Paint needs to dry thoroughly between coats. To avoid washing your brush/applicator, wrap it in kitchen foil—this stops the paint drying and your brush is ready to be used again for the second coat. Don't forget to put the lid back on your paint can.

You can see here what a difference a second coat makes—on the right, the color is stronger and you can't see the wood anymore.

Diluting paint When you just want a hint of color on your wood, diluting your paint is a good option.

1 Water-based paints are the easiest to dilute. In a container mix together equal quantities of paint and water. Give it a good stir, then use a brush to check the color on a test piece of wood. If you think it is too dark, add more water until you have the right shade.

2 You can see the difference between normal and diluted paint above—the top piece of wood has had two coats of normal paint, while the bottom piece has had one coat of diluted paint with a 50/50 mix of paint/water.

Cleaning paintbrushes

Water-based paint can be rinsed out of your brushes by holding them under slightly warm running water. Work your fingers through the brush to get all the paint out. When the water runs clear, you're finished. Let the brush dry before you store it away.

Oil-based paints need to be removed with white spirit. Place some spirit in a container (such as an old glass jar). Work the white spirit into the bristles; when you are sure your brush is clean, rinse the brush in warm water.

Cleaning your brushes correctly after painting will prolong their life, but bear in mind that a foam applicator can only be washed and reused a couple of times.

How to wallpaper

It doesn't matter what you paper—a piece of canvas like my wallpaper painting on page 13, a door, or just a wall—the method is the same. You put glue on the surface and stick paper against it.

1 Here I wallpapered an alcove with a brick-patterned paper. Mix up the wallpaper paste according to the packet instructions. Using the paste brush, apply a layer of wallpaper paste to the surface you want to paper.

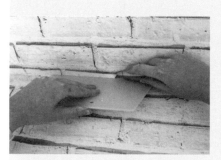

3 Hold the wallpaper smoother on the bottom edge of your surface and run the Stanley knife along its edge to cut the paper.

It may look tricky, but it is actually very easy. You will need a plastic container (or bucket if papering a large area), wallpaper paste, Stanley knife and scissors, paste brush, smoothing brush, and a wallpaper smoother.

2 Push the paper against the top edge of the area being papered, making sure it is straight. Using the smoothing brush and working from the middle outward, smooth out all air bubbles under the paper. If necessary, use the wallpaper smoother to smooth the edges.

4 You need to match the pattern on your next wallpaper piece so the seam is unnoticeable, and it is easier to do this before you apply paste to the wall. Find where the match is and mark it lightly with a pencil, then apply paste and stick the paper to the surface. Trim the top of the paper once it is in place.

CRAFTING MATERIALS

If you're a crafter, you're likely to have a lot of these materials in your stash already.

PAPER

Magazine sheets (1) Also called tear sheets. Photos or images torn from magazines are great to use for decoupage.

Washi tape (2) My favorite craft material! Use to decorate wood, create picture frames on walls, and decorate envelopes, among many other uses.

Varnish glue (3) Once dry, this water-based varnish creates a transparent, shiny, non-sticky, and water-resistant film over paper.

You will also need:

• Paper scissors (4)

FABRICS AND YARNS

Outdoor fabric (5) This is cotton treated with a chemical to make the fabric waterproof. It is thick and strong, but a bit harder to sew.

Upholstery fabric (6) This tough, durable fabric can withstand heavy wear. The higher the thread count (number of threads per square inch), the more tightly woven the fabric is, and the better it will wear.

Indoor fabric (7) You can use any kind of fabric indoors. I like using cottons for my projects.

Fabric dye (8) This comes in powdered or liquid form. Follow the manufacturer's instructions for use. Great for changing the colors of sofa covers, bedding, or curtains.

Jersey yarn (9) A great upcycled product using leftover fabric from the clothing industry (see page 19).

Needles (10) These come in lots of different sizes. Straight needles are good for hand sewing pillows and the more delicate your fabric, the thinner the needle. Upholstery and curved needles are good for sewing carpet squares together.

You will also need:

• Twine (11)
• Cotton thread (12)
• Yarn (13)
• Pins (14)
• Tape measure (15)
• Fabric scissors (16)
• Fabric marker (17)
• Sewing machine

RESOURCES

Hester van Overbeek
www.hestershandmadehome.com
www.youtube.com/handmadehome
Instagram: byhestergrams
Twitter: @hestershandmade

RECOMMENDED STORES AND RESOURCES

Furniture
If you don't already have a piece of furniture you'd like to transform, take a look at your local furniture market or car boot sale/yard sale, or have a look online. I found most of my pieces at Scotts's Furniture Mart.
www.scottsmargate.co.uk

You could also try:
www.ebay.com
www.preloved.com
www.freecycle.org
www.gumtree.com

I'm a big fan of Scandinavian design and where else to buy this on a budget than at Ikea.
www.ikea.com

Paint
For all the large pieces of furniture I used milk paints from General Finishes, which comes in beautiful colors and is super easy to apply.
www.eurofinishes.com
www.generalfinishes.com

For a more matte or distressed finish, I like using Annie Sloan's Chalk Paint®. This doesn't require any preparation like sanding and priming—what's not to love?
www.anniesloan.com

Patterned power cable
As used in the project on page 64.
www.cultfurniture.com (UK)
www.colorcord.com

DIY
I always check the wood I have in my shed before buying anything new—you'll be surprised what you can make from offcuts or leftover cupboards. If you need new materials, have a look at your local lumber/timber merchants, as they often have inexpensive, quality wood.

I'm lucky to live near the brilliant H.E. Harrington (tel. +44 (0) 1843 862 091). Whatever you ask for, somewhere in the shop will be exactly what you requested. For bigger things, try superstores:
www.diy.com
www.homebase.co.uk
www.homedepot.com

The wallpaper for the wallpaper painting on page 10 is from Mini Moderns. They have a great selection of not only wallpapers but also fabrics, paints, and furnishings.
www.minimoderns.com

Fabric
As well as using my local fabric store, I also love to buy fabrics online. My favorites are M is for Make and Clarke&Clarke. eBay and Amazon are also great sources for fabrics.
www.misformake.co.uk
www.clarke-clarke.com

I love working with Zpagetti yarn from Hoooked, as they use leftover cotton products from the clothing industry. They ship worldwide.
www.hoooked.nl

For wool or cotton yarns, have a look at LoveKnitting or Purl Soho.
www.loveknitting.com
www.purlsoho.com

Interior and homewares
I love West Elm and some of the pictures in this book are styled with their beautiful products. West Elm make it very easy to decorate your home in their modern, chic style with ethnic touches.
www.westelm.com/.co.uk

For a bit of Dutch influence, I like Hema. They sell everything you'll ever need from cool home decorations to stationery, coffee pots to bicycles. They also sell the best washi tape around. Shops can be found in every town in Holland, and now across Europe, too, but luckily for us they also ship abroad.
www.hemashop.com

Anthropologie sell the best quirky home accessories and artifacts from around the globe.
www.anthropologie.com

For budget friendly prices, go to H&M home.
www.hm.com

Websites and magazines
I'm a magazine junkie, and now you can read foreign magazines online, my obsession is getting worse. Here are some of my favorite magazine websites and blogs:

www.pinterest.com—I love browsing for tips and ideas.

www.relovedmag.co.uk—full of upcycled ideas and tips. I often design and write projects for them.

www.brightbazaarblog.com—Will has a keen eye for color and will make you want to transform your home into a color paradise.

www.abeautifulmess.com—Elsie and Emma have such a fresh and unique approach to home décor and